An illustrated souvenir

FARNE ISLANDS

Northumberland

The National Trust

Introduction

The Inner Farne stack

The Farne Islands vary in number from about fifteen to twenty-eight, depending on the state of the tide. They consist of two main groups, the inner and the outer, separated by the mile-wide Staple Sound, and two outliers, Crumstone to the east and Megstone to the west. The principal island, Inner Farne, is some 6.7 hectares (16½ acres) in extent and includes 4.4 hectares (about 11 acres) of bare rock; other major islands are Staple Island, Brownsman, East and West Wideopens, North and South Wamses, Big and Little Harcar and the Longstone.

They are the most easterly point on the outcrop of the Great Whin Sill, a formation that runs for some 70–80 miles across the north of England. The whin is an intrusive sheet of hard dolerite and the resultant scenery provides suitable nesting habitat for many different species of seabird. The general trend of the rock is from south-west to north-east and this means that the islands have cliffs, or rocky faces, on the south and west and slope gradually to the north and east. The cliffs reach a height of 21–24 m near the Inner Farne lighthouse.

Puffins line the south cliff of Inner Farne

Sandwich terns rise in a cloud above the sea campion on Inner Farne

3

Plants

Amsinckia intermedia

Thrift

The whin is everywhere more or less deeply fissured and in certain places the fissures are very well developed and give rise to such features as Kittiwake Gully on Staple Island, and the Churn blowhole on Inner Farne. Its columnar nature is shown clearly in the isolated rock stack near Inner Farne and the Pinnacles group off Staple Island. There are only three sandy beaches, the most extensive being that in St Cuthbert's Cove. Striae on the whin show clearly the effect of glacial action, but the most important result of glaciation was the deposition of boulder clay on Brownsman, Staple Island, Inner Farne and West Wideopens. On top of this clay subsoil is a layer of light peat and it is here that virtually all the vegetation is found.

There are no trees and the only shrubs are a few stunted elder bushes on Inner Farne. Sea campion is the characteristic plant and, in summer, its white flowers cover much of Inner Farne, Staple Island and Brownsman. Some 116 species of plant have been recorded, the majority on Inner Farne; they include thrift, scurvy grass, ragwort, silverweed, bugloss, sorrel, nettle and dock. Most interesting, however, is a kind of borage, *Amsinckia intermedia*. This is a native of Lower California and was probably introduced many years ago when the lightkeepers kept poultry here.

Staple Island showing some of the characteristic features of the whin

St Cuthbert

For nearly 900 years hermits and monks lived on Inner Farne, the best known being St Cuthbert who was born about 637. After twelve years as Prior of Lindisfarne, he retired to Inner Farne in 678, remaining there until 684 when he became Bishop of Lindisfarne. His health deteriorated and in December 686 he returned to Inner Farne where he died on 20 March 687. Although he was buried in Durham, his influence remained and for centuries this island was a place of pilgrimage.

Several of the later hermits came from the Convent of Durham and in 1246 a small daughter community, the House of Farne, was established: there were usually only two monks, the Master and the Associate, together with one or two servants.

With the exception of the lighthouse, all the buildings on Inner Farne date from the monastic period. St Cuthbert had provided a hospitium for his visitors and the monks subsequently built a guest house on the site: all that now remains is the small stone 'Fishehouse' near the landing place.

Stone coffin, believed to be that of Thomas Sparowe, one of the Masters of the House of Farne (c.1430)

The monastic buildings, including the 'Fishehouse', from St Cuthbert's Cove

St Cuthbert's chapel showing the galilee. The font was brought by Archdeacon Thorp from Gateshead parish church

A contrast in woodwork: 17th-century stalls from Durham Cathedral and 20th-century mouse, carved by Mr Thompson on the altar cross

Interior of St Cuthbert's chapel, showing part of the 17th-century woodwork; some of the angel heads were cut off by minesweeper crews during the 1914–18 war. The one remaining 14th-century window is now filled in and is only visible from outside

There were two chapels, but that dedicated to St Mary has virtually disappeared. The present chapel was completed in 1370 and the little galilee at the west end is typical of buildings associated with St Cuthbert. By 1840 it was roofless, and its existence today is largely due to the restoration work carried out by the Ven. Charles Thorp, Archdeacon of Durham, who purchased the inner group of islands in 1861. A striking feature of the interior is the fine seventeenth-century woodwork: this had been removed from Durham Cathedral in 1848 and was saved from possible destruction by Archdeacon Thorp. The east window dates from 1844 and contains glass by William Wailes of Newcastle. The wooden altar furnishings carry a tiny mouse, trademark of their maker, 'Mousey' Thompson.

The tower was built in about 1500 by Thomas Castell, one of the priors of Durham, and probably occupies the site of St Cuthbert's cell. After the dissolution of the monastery in 1536 the Farnes were granted to the Dean and Chapter of Durham and in 1673 the first official lighthouse was established when a fire was lit nightly on top of the tower.

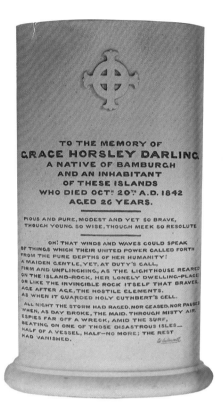

Grace Darling's memorial in
St Cuthbert's chapel

Lighthouses

The first purpose-built lighthouse was a square tower
erected on Staple Island. Here, too, a beacon fire was
used and when the tower was destroyed in 1783 another
tower was built on Brownsman.

In 1809, the first modern lighthouse was constructed
on Inner Farne and in 1810 a similar tower was put up
on Brownsman. Unfortunately, this proved a danger to
shipping and in 1826 it was replaced by a lighthouse on
the Longstone. The Brownsman light was afterwards
demolished.

The name of Grace Darling will always be linked with
the Longstone lighthouse. Her grandfather, Robert, was
appointed keeper on Brownsman in 1795; he was
followed, in 1815, by his son William, and the Darlings
subsequently moved to the Longstone. The most famous
of all Farne wrecks, that of SS *Forfarshire*, took place on
7 September 1838. The steamer struck the west corner
of Big Harcar and Grace and her father rowed from the
Longstone, in appalling conditions, to rescue five
survivors. As a result, she became a national heroine, but
she died of tuberculosis in 1842 when only twenty-six.

The old beacon lighthouse on
Staple Island

The Inner Farne lighthouse is built on the
highest point of the islands

Management

The monks made considerable use of the resources of the islands, and after 1536, when they were let to various tenants, this exploitation continued. By the 1840s, the continued existence of the seabird colonies was seriously threatened, but fortunately Archdeacon Thorp decided to employ wardens during the breeding season. This proved very effective in safeguarding the birds, and similar measures were adopted by the Farne Islands Association, an organisation founded in 1881 by local bird lovers. As a result, the islands have been a bird sanctuary for over a century.

The outer group was bought by Lord Armstrong in 1912, and in 1925, following a public appeal, both groups were purchased and handed over to the National Trust. The Farnes are now one of the most important nature reserves in Europe and the Trust has introduced an overall management plan which ensures that all who come there – seals, birds and human visitors – can get the maximum benefit from their stay without in any way endangering the habitat.

The cottage and ruined lighthouses on Brownsman

Sea campion on the top of Staple Island contrasts with the bare, fissured whin which forms much of the island

The south-east cliff of Brownsman with the Longstone lighthouse in the background. The camera has considerably foreshortened the distance between the islands

General

At least 274 species of bird have been recorded from the Farnes. Many of these are summer migrants on passage, while in autumn thousands of incoming winter visitors sometimes appear. A few flocks of waders – dunlins, turnstones and purple sandpipers – are present throughout the year.

The islands are, however, best known for breeding seabirds, and fifteen species – fulmars, cormorants, shags, eiders, gulls, terns and auks – as well as small numbers of ringed plovers, oystercatchers and rock pipits, nest each year. Birds that have occasionally nested include shelducks, mallards, moorhens, lapwings, redshanks, common and great black-backed gulls, meadow pipits, pied wagtails, stonechats, wheatears, blackbirds, jackdaws, carrion crows and starlings.

Oystercatchers. Between twenty and thirty pairs nest each year and large flocks are seen in spring and autumn

Fulmars first nested in 1935 and there are now over 250 pairs

The Pinnacles, isolated rock stacks off
Staple Island

Eiders

St Cuthbert was the first person in this country to carry out bird protection, for he had a particular affection for eider ducks and laid down rules for their welfare during the breeding season. Medieval writers described their tameness, saying that they could be handled without showing fear, while some even laid their eggs in houses. Much of this is still true and between 1,000 and 2,000 ducks now nest, the majority on Inner Farne. They are usually found among vegetation, or against the old drystone walls, but many odd sites are chosen and two or three often nest against the chapel and tower, within a very short distance of visitors. Perhaps the strangest site was underneath the wooden seat outside the chapel where the duck below, and the wardens above, were all 'sitting comfortably'.

Eiders are present around the islands throughout the year and the black and white drakes are at their most handsome in spring. However, they are not attentive mates, for although they help to choose the nesting site, they remain there for only a short time. Instead, when the ducklings are hatched, the drake's duties may be taken over by an 'aunt', a non-breeding duck which helps the youngsters to reach the sea.

Nesting eider duck

A drake eider spends only a short time with his mate

Mother and 'aunt'. Eiders and ducklings on the Churn pool, Inner Farne

Cormorants and shags

Like eiders, cormorants and shags are seen throughout the year although many local shags move south in winter, being replaced by birds from further north. Cormorants have been residents for centuries with breeding colonies on Megstone, North Wamses and, less frequently, Little Harcar and East Wideopens. Today, the 250 or so pairs are on the Wamses and East Wideopens. Megstone has been deserted since 1973. A visit to a cormorant island is not for the squeamish: the rocks are running with limewash, the whole area is covered with decaying fish and the smell is indescribable. The nests are made of seaweed, but sometimes incorporate such unusual objects as a baby's comforter or rabbit's skull.

A fifteenth-century list of the Farne Islands includes the 'Scarphcarrs', a name obviously derived from 'scarf', a cormorant or shag, and the Scarcars are still a favourite resting place for these birds. In the past, a few pairs of shags bred occasionally, but since 1931 they have nested annually: there are now over 1,000 pairs, over half of them on Staple Island.

Fulmars are fairly recent arrivals: they were first reported in 1919, but it was not until 1935 that a pair nested on Inner Farne. Numbers increased gradually and about 250 pairs are scattered over nine or ten islands. (They lay a single egg, on bare ground, and if this is lost do not replace it.)

Part of the North Wamses cormorant colony

Nesting shag showing the distinctive crest

Queen of the castle! An unusual cormorant's nest, about a metre high

Gulls

Most attractive of the gulls are the kittiwakes whose tameness makes them a photographer's delight, while their continuous call of 'kitti-wa-a-ke, kitti-wa-a-ke' is a characteristic summer sound. There are over 6,000 pairs, and their cup-shaped nests are literally stuck on to the cliff faces where they make use of even the tiniest projection of rock. In winter they spread out over the seas – indeed, birds from the Farnes were the first known to have crossed the Atlantic – sometimes even penetrating into the Mediterranean.

The predatory lesser black-backed and herring gulls are far from welcome residents. They nest mainly on rocky islands with comparatively little vegetation, such as the Wamses, Harcars and Wideopens and, in the past, many hundreds of eggs were collected by local fishermen. Despite this, numbers continued to increase – they rose from 2,776 pairs in 1972 to 5,284 pairs in 1974 – and measures are now taken to keep them in check. Black-headed gulls were once a rare breeding species, but recently they have been nesting in increasing numbers near the tern colonies.

Kittiwake Gully, Staple Island

Gulls and terns near the Churn pool,
Inner Farne

Kittiwake and young

Terns

Four species of terns nest, the majority on Inner Farne and Brownsman, and it is an unforgettable sight when these graceful birds dive and wheel against a blue sky. Memorable, too, is an arctic tern's dive-bombing attack, as it defends its nest from the unwary visitor.

There are usually 2,000–3,000 pairs of Sandwich terns, but they are temperamental birds and it is impossible to predict where they will settle. By contrast, arctic terns usually return to their birthplace and, indeed, one was still nesting there after twenty-eight years. Some 1,500–4,000 pairs are on both Inner Farne and Brownsman, but there are seldom more than 150–250 pairs of common terns. Rarest of all is the beautiful roseate tern, for although there were nearly a hundred nests in 1953, there are now fewer than five.

All the terns winter thousands of miles to the south, mainly off the coasts of Africa, although one arctic tern was found in New South Wales – only the third British tern to reach Australia!

Young arctic tern

Arctic tern. Some 3,000–4,000 pairs nest, mainly on Inner Farne and Brownsman

Terns flying over the Kettle, Inner Farne. West Wideopens can be seen in the background

Auks

Tradition says that in the mid eighteenth century a great auk was captured alive on the Farnes and subsequently became a household pet. Great auks are, alas, extinct, but three species of auk still nest here, while black and Brunnich's guillemots, and little auks, appear occasionally.

Guillemots crowd the tops of the Pinnacles, and others are on Staple Island, Brownsman, North Wamses, Megstone, Inner Farne and the Wideopens. Countless thousands of guillemots have died as the result of oiling, but fortunately Farne birds seem largely to have escaped the major disasters; they have increased steadily so that over 19,000 pairs now breed compared with about 1,350 in 1971. Some 4 per cent of Farne birds are 'bridled', i.e. they have a white ring round their eye: this compares with less than 1 per cent on the south coast of England and 50 per cent in Spitzbergen.

There are comparatively few razorbills, although here, too, numbers are increasing. For many years there were less than a dozen pairs, but over 100 pairs now nest while other, non-breeding birds are also present round the islands. Both guillemots and razorbills lay their single egg on bare rock, but the latter are solitary rather than communal nesters, and prefer a ledge to themselves.

A bridled guillemot joins the razorbills

Guillemots crowd together off Staple Island

Puffin burrows among the sea campion

Few people realize that the puffin is the most numerous nesting bird of the Farnes – there are about 34,000 pairs! They are found wherever there is sufficient depth of soil for their burrows, with the largest colonies on Staple Island, Brownsman and West Wideopens. They are attractive little birds and the name 'sea parrot' aptly describes their brightly coloured beak, a beak which, while ideal for carrying sand eels, can produce an extremely painful bite. They lay a single egg, and in a wet season, when many of the burrows are flooded, there is a high mortality among the young.

Ringing has shown that there is a definite interchange between puffin colonies, especially with the Isle of May, off Fife. It has also proved that puffins and guillemots are long-lived – Farne birds have reached 23 and 25 years respectively! Both species suffered considerably in the last century; despite difficulty of access, guillemots' eggs were gathered regularly from the Pinnacles, and there was a particularly inhuman incident in 1875 when the vegetation on Staple Island was deliberately set on fire, and the puffins burnt alive in their burrows.

Many thousands of birds, among them puffins, are ringed each year

Seals

With the exception of rabbits, grey seals are the only mammals found on the Farne Islands; they have been here for at least 800 years and the colony is one of the most important in the British Isles. All visitors to the islands want to 'see the seals' and, fortunately, the seals cooperate, for they are inquisitive animals and often come quite close to a boat to inspect its passengers. Moreover, at low tide many of them haul out on to the rocks – huge bulls, which can measure up to 3 m in length, smaller mottled cows and fawnish-brown youngsters. They lie in all sorts of curious positions, often huddled closely together, and occasionally one will yawn or lift a fore-flipper to scratch itself.

Most of the young are born in late October/November, the main nursery islands being the North and South Wamses and the Northern Hares. Each cow has a single pup which at birth is covered with soft white hair, about 3 cm long; this is gradually moulted so that at four weeks old the pup has a much shorter, greyish coat. Seals' milk is very rich and in two or three weeks the slim newborn pup (it weighs only $13\frac{1}{2}$kg) becomes a round little barrel. A few days later it goes to sea and from then on has to live on its fat and fend for itself. Some pups leave the islands, dispersing over many hundreds of miles, and they have been found, often when only a few weeks old, in Norway, Sweden, Germany and Holland, as well as along the coasts of Britain.

In the past, seals were regarded as an important source of oil and skins and they were killed regularly on the islands. However, they have been protected for over a century and, as a result, they increased steadily from about a hundred in the early 1900s to some 7,000 in 1970. In the 1990s the colony stabilised at some 3,500 animals, producing around 1,000 pups annually. In severe autumn storms, mortality among the pups can be 50 per cent.

A slim little white-coated youngster

Within a short time the newborn calf becomes a round little barrel

Seals hauled out on the rocks